How to Become a Stripper

The Ultimate Guide to Becoming an Exotic Dancer and Making Lots of Money

by Ali Donahue

Table of Contents

Introduction

You've probably heard of college students stripping part-time to cover the cost of their tuition, and for good reason: You can make a ton of money in a short period of time, and you don't need any work experience at all to get the job. The only deterrent really is the social stigma, but if you can get past that, then stripping is a great way to earn a significant income, whether as a part-time side job, or even as your full-time career. Sure, stripping isn't for everyone, but if you're considering it or on the fence about whether or not it might be right for you, then this book is going to give you a lot of valuable insight that will help you make up your mind.

Although the basic premise of stripping or "exotic dancing" has historical evidence spanning past millennia—as can be surmised from the biblical tale of Salome's dance before Herod Antipas (called "Dance of the Seven Veils" in Oscar Wilde's play), and even dating further back to figurines of erotic dancers from roughly 8500 years go—the advent of payment in exchange for this form of entertainment, traditionally linked to hospitality, has provided a means for determined men and women to earn a generous income, while they pursue other vocations and avocations – if they so desire.

However, while most novices expect stripping to be an easy source of money, it has to be emphasized that this is a job like any other, with one exception: Success isn't defined by how much money you make while in it, but rather how soon you are able to earn enough money so that you can leave it. Yes, while this claim may be slightly presumptuous, every successful stripper out there is regarded so, not because of their looks, body, or earnings per night, but because he or she diligently planned and prepared for the day when this life would be left behind for greener pastures. So, instead of throwing it all away, to be financially successful in this business, you must chalk out the framework for a disciplined life which will use the riches from stripping to ensure that, soon enough, you never have to work again.

Also, while we're on this topic, it must be mentioned that novices often enter this life with visions of money raining down on them as if US Treasury Mint trucks got drunk and regurgitated green bills like freshmen at their first drink-till-you-drop party. The reality is far from so. Like any other entrepreneurial or self-employed field, there are pitfalls to navigate and habits to employ which will make your life easier and earnings considerably greater. And until you do so, and put in the hard work, effort, and physically grueling dedication this life *demands*, chances are you'll probably end up *owing* money rather than making it.

So, if you're ready to learn the ins and outs of the stripping industry and how to ensure that you'll be financially successful, then let's get started!

Chapter 1: Primary and Secondary Skills You'll Need, and the To-Dos of Stripping

As with every other profession, stripping has skills which have direct or indirect bearing on your success in professional endeavors. Within exotic dancing, those skills aren't limited to dancing itself, but range across a variety of subtle talents that deal with everything from salesmanship to an understanding of body language.

Though popular culture often depicts strippers as either drop-dead gorgeous or worn down and raggedy, successful strippers aren't dependent on looks but rather their aura of sensuality. That said, let's at least take care of the basics and get yourself in reasonable shape. Fitness not only boosts confidence, allowing you to display your nakedness with more flair when required, but also increases endurance—which is rather important. This isn't the job for you if you can't stand or dance around for hours on end in extremely uncomfortable stilettos.

Along with fitness also comes the need to be comfortable in your own skin, rather literally in this case. While you're still standing in your bedroom, one of the most crucial things becomes practicing minor details such as your walk, your role, and the looks which you maintain upon your pretty face. If you are one of those people who have spent the majority of their lives *in* their clothing rather than out of it so far, having to openly display large portions of your assets, while drawing the least amount of attention to your innate shyness or any discomfort with that state of affairs, can throw you off your game. Not only would this affect the sensuality and seductiveness of your dance or walk, but severely hamper the smolders in your look that would have otherwise set you apart from the other strippers in the club.

Therefore, once you've taken the decision to take up stripping, practice walking in your chosen outfits at home in various stages of undress to acclimatize yourself with the feel of your nudity. However, this won't help you if you live with your parents or other roommates in front of whom such behavior would be considered inappropriate. In these cases, choose other locations such as beaches or swimming pools where skimpy clothing is appropriate, and practice walking around in your smallest clothes and bikinis under the gaze of others. Retain your class and elegance in these practice walks, because the biggest objective of this exercise is to acclimatize yourself with your body on display under the piercing gaze of onlookers.

In fact, you can turn this situation to your advantage by practicing different walks and gauging its effects on the people in your surroundings. If you're emotionally attached or part of a couple, I would recommend leaving the smoldering looks out of this exercise altogether lest you deeply offend your partner, but coming up with and testing different walks shouldn't leave your better half with any unpleasant emotions.

Another skill which needs practice before hitting the stage is your make-up, and this doesn't mean obsessing over tiny flaws in your skin. The dark lighting, and even the occasional spotlights on your stage performance in some clubs, is intended to dampen down and even whitewash the small flaws in every performer's skin or features. Use that to your advantage, and instead use your make-up to imbue more sexual energy in your basic look. The one thing which needs to be kept in mind is the key difference between stripper make-up and everyday or going out make-up. Without being garish or trashy, strippers often need to use slightly heavier make-up than that of everyday life since the lighting schemes tend to tone it all down regardless—which is something most stage performers need to get used to through practice alone.

Beyond these basic skills, you also need to create and perfect your persona. This doesn't just affect your basic personality traits while you're at a strip club, but also the role you play while stripping. If you think that stripping is about taking your clothes off to some music, you are way off base. The most successful strippers don't do well just because they turn the act of undressing into an art form, but rather because they do so within a character—the naughty nurse, sexy yet stern police officer, helpless innocent girl, etc. While patrons at strip clubs are often satisfied with the act of undressing leading to the novelty of nudity as well, this particular *novelty* disappears **fast**— leaving them to pursue strippers who provide them the added bonus of spicing up or playing out their fantasies as well. On the other hand, strippers who concentrate specifically on providing the rather two-dimensional service of blandly undressing and gyrating on-stage often find themselves at the lower end of the earning pole. So, pick a role which suits you the best or even intrigues you the most, and suit yourself up accordingly.

Along with the clothes, you also need to prepare a personality that would complement the role you pick. This personality will not only decide your character traits while you work—smiling and peppy, reserved and sultry, mysterious and bold, etc.—but also a fake name and background for yourself. Always flesh this particular bit out as much as possible since there will be many instances where you will be asked about your personal life by clients. In this situation, if you try to swiftly and harshly put boundaries in place, it may work well but it will also make you considerably less desirable to your clients—which means less money through work and tips.

When deciding upon a name and background, many strippers also put a romantic history in place in order to dissuade particularly pushy customers. Again, though you may call for the bouncer to handle the situation for you, it means less money for you through tips from these particular clients and any others who may have overheard or seen this exchange. Customers may sometimes get out of hand, and the ability to handle such instances discretely often determines the popularity of one great stripper among many other talented ones. In this regard, female strippers often say that they're bisexual by orientation and are currently involved with another woman. This response keeps male customers on the hook since they need to genuinely *believe* that you're attracted to them in some way, and yet dissuades them from making any overt moves for your affection as it were.

Apart from the preparations outlined above, successful strippers also invest greatly in their talents on-stage. Although they make much more money in tips and VIP rooms off-stage, the platform is a great way for strippers to enchant would-be loyal customers through their own sensual charm and wiles. Therefore, dance forms such as pole dancing are a given in this line. Strippers sign up for classes like these to separate themselves from the amateur riff-raff that lines most stages, and to distinguish themselves within the herd. Since customers are a common pool from which strippers win their bread-and-butter regulars, being able to heighten your sexuality through your dance is a necessary advantage lest some other colleague wins them over first.

In keeping with that line of thought, many successful strippers also tend to broaden their dancing horizons by schooling themselves in other less traditional dance forms—such as belly dancing, Kizomba, Lambada, etc. By integrating the skills learnt from other such dance forms into their pole-dancing routine, they are able to visibly distinguish their own dances from the others in a club, while feeling even sexier on the pole themselves.

The next skill that all successful strippers must have is the ability to communicate clearly and eloquently. While you don't need to sound as if William Wordsworth was your father, it does help if strippers are well-spoken and well-mannered in their approach to clientele. The largest customers for most strippers are often business people—some aiming to butter up clients before closing a deal, while others simply wish to dissociate themselves from a miserable day—and so showing elegance and class in the way you talk, and not just the way you walk, may make you the favorite to whom they regularly bring their preferred business.

Along with better communication skills also comes the need to be a great listener. Most money made by strippers through their regulars isn't on tips or lap dances, but rather through talking and listening to their customers. These people just want the attention of a man or woman they consider attractive, and to possibly purge the weight of their problems through them. Therefore, being able to give your client your undivided attention, listening to their problems with sincerity, and being able to discuss solutions when you're able are often marks of a great stripper.

Chapter 2: How to Choose the Best Club

The world of the professional stripping is a rather weirdly structured one—and yet, that ultimately works heavily in your favor. The way a stripper works is through a club, where you pay a house fee per shift *when* you choose to work there. Apart from the most exclusive establishments, most clubs host auditions once a week for talented amateurs and established industry professionals alike. And the placement and nature of a stripper's first club often has a significant effect on the take-home earnings as well as future career upswings experienced by the stripper.

Beyond that long-term effect that you might suffer if you pick a bad establishment as your first taste, the other short-term problem is the sort of club which ignores operations within its walls enough for most of its strippers to comfortably provide "extras"—such activities that are banned through the letter of the law, the rules of the club, or the rules of the stripping industry at large. These may involve either "turning tricks" through prostitution or even something like acting out a fantasy for a customer without engaging in any direct sexual favors. Whatever may be the case here, if too many of the strippers regularly and comfortably break the law by indulging in prostitution or acting as escorts, even outside the club, to customers that they pick up within its walls, the establishment is likely to get caught up in a Vice raid, and you'll be swept away right along with it.

Last, but definitely not the least, come the sleaziest sort of clubs—ones that use shifty and convolutedly worded legal contracts that trap strippers through large cuts in pay, enforcing a cycle of debt to the establishment when certain amounts of money aren't forthcoming, resulting in a modern-day legally sanctioned version of financial slavery. Once you're caught up in this sort of operation, you're at the mercy of the establishment itself. And then, the picture of your immediate future becomes quite dependent on the character and mercy of the ones holding your leash—which, if it were pristine, would never have resulted in this situation to begin with. Unless you wish to see yourself trading one "favor" after another in exchange for reducing paltry sums of money from what seems like a life sentence of debt that was never initiated by you, keep your eyes *peeled* for this sort of racket. It happens more often than you think.

Now, after this long-winded warning, let's discuss the actual mechanics behind choosing a good club. In today's day and age, almost every establishment— except for the sleaziest ones, which is probably a good thing—have their own websites, as well as local websites that compare the strip clubs within cities based on quality, cleanliness, service, security, etc., and those will be the handiest tools for you.

Once you've selected a large array of clubs within which you would find comfortable working conditions at first glance, give each of them a call and inquire about the next call for auditions. The way these work is that mediocre to low-earning potential clubs keep open auditions where you can go at any time, or on two to three days in the week, try out on stage, and start working from the next day if you choose to do so. Establishments which are more upscale host auditions once a week or fortnight instead. As you move further up the scale, you run into different clubs—from those which need you to have a known profile and reputation within a few clubs for you to try out there, to ones which only allow you to audition by invitation, and ending with the most exclusive ones—where you don't necessarily have to pay a house fee and will be paid instead by the club to show up and entertain. That explains why you'd need to have a certain level of repute within the industry, and need to have worked with several upscale establishments before, etc.

As you may have guessed, your opening acts will thus be mediocre clubs at best—and this is why you need to be extremely careful about your final choice. Once you've received the green light for auditions, you're required to go over and give a basic interview where your skills (if any, since many beginners are absolute amateurs) and assets (shape, firmness, aesthetic appeal of your various physical endowments) will be gauged. You may be required to display your comfort with nudity by performing as such for a while or even just standing or twirling on the spot for the manager or any other member of the establishment who may be handling the auditions.

Either during the auditions, or while the powers-that-be are deliberating their decision, try to meet the house mom, floor manager, bouncer, or even DJ if you can. There are no distinctions in importance among these house personnel, since each of them will contribute to your success in a definitive manner. The house mom—regardless of gender—is usually the one who takes care of all a stripper's needs behind closed curtains. From providing make-up to small snacks and sweets when needed, the house mom is the answer to every need a stripper may have while working. The floor manager greets and directs customers to different sections. As with most talented strippers, floor managers have plenty of experience with cold-reading people who enter the club, and so can decently distinguish people who would probably end up being bigger spenders than others. A friendly floor manager makes all the difference between whether you make plenty of moola, or end up owing the club each night.

The bouncer is your protector and final line of defense. From keeping drunk clientele at bay when all other attempts fail, to escorting you to your car each night to keep you safe, the bouncer is your best friend at the worst of times. A cordial relationship or lack thereof with this part of the staff decides whether he willingly protects you or turns a blind eye to a patron's misbehavior with you—or worse, if you're already outside the club. The DJ holds the biggest key to a successful performance—the music. A DJ who's in your corner will do his best to either match his music to your moves, or will happily accept specific music requests from you to help you up your earning intake. A hostile one will simply implode the entire event by playing tunes which simply *do not* let you get into your own groove. Get a feel for each of these staff members, and try to build an early rapport with them even before you've signed a contract.

Once they've approved of your physical attributes and other qualities for the place, they will probably provide you with a contract applicable to their club. This may not always be the case either, since some would just tell you to show up the next day and pick whichever shifts you'd like to work, or even tell you to work for a certain number of days regularly before you're allowed to start picking your shift times and days. Whichever the case may be, if there is any paper at all which you're required to sign, take it back home and read it. If it's an honest(-ish) establishment, then it would have no trouble letting you do so regardless and would in fact appreciate your dedication to understanding the rules.

If they throw a hissy fit, or try to bully or rush you into signing a paper, take that as a **massive** red flag. Even if they say that it's the last position available, and if you don't sign right away, they won't consider your application—do not sign right there. In fact, don't even offer to stay there and read before signing, since the emotional atmosphere they create within the interview will push you into a corner where you may end up signing just to get it over with and start working.

Only once you've gone home and perused through the contract or legal document with a fine-toothed comb should you think about signing it and returning to that establishment the next day. Some legal contracts may even have exclusivity or non-compete clauses inserted within them. The first sort states that you can't perform at any other establishment in the city or state if you choose to work at their establishment, for as long as you work there. The second sort states that if you stop working at their club for any reason, you may not dance at any other establishment for a certain length of time. An exclusivity clause may work out if you're joining a decent establishment and everything else seems to check out about them. The advantage of being a stripper, however, is the freedom to approach several clubs—so don't give that freedom away lightly and choose the ones that work in your favor, allowing you to set your own work hours and days.

After having deliberated on the legality of the contract, and whether or not its terms are acceptable to you, think back to your meeting with the various house personnel. If you've given multiple auditions—which I strongly recommend before finalizing a decision—choose the club which not only has the best working terms for you, but one which additionally has the most supportive or professional staff (those two terms don't usually even remotely denote the same group of people, but either one or the other is still good).

Chapter 3: The Persona of a Successful Stripper

While there isn't a single overriding set of characteristics which define successful strippers, there are some qualities which are shared between them. Though successful exotic dancers may be chirpy, serious, exuberant, or any other quality within the entire spectrum, they're all extremely disciplined.

Most strippers manage to fall into a few categories—broke, part-time, junkie, and money whiz, to name a few. Now before you go jumping to conclusions, the names of these categories reflect truths much deeper than what can be gleaned at first glance.

The broke stripper isn't one who never has any money, but one who may even have a lot of money but blows it all on parties, booze, drugs, clothes, shoes, and other short-term pleasures. Given the nature of this business, they live a fairly hand-to-mouth existence where they keep inflating their lifestyle based on their last earnings, without any thought to their future. Since the problem is that strippers rarely experience success beyond the age of 28 to 30, they will find themselves in deep waters at every turn of their life unless they drastically alter their attitude towards money and responsibilities.

The part-time strippers are the ones who use this profession to supplement their earnings or other secondary sources of income, while they actively pursue other interests. The most common example of this type is the student stripper. Since they're visitors to this industry, their success isn't defined by their performance in it. However, they also have some of the worst work ethic in the industry, and only seldom pose any sort of competition to established and successful strippers.

The junkie stripper has nothing to do with drugs, though many strippers from the first category do land nose-first into drug issues. The junkie stripper is the smallest subset of the lot, and refers to the tiny group of men and women who take to stripping as a means of getting their jollies. These people truly enjoy the experience, for many diverse reasons, and may sometimes delve into it with such vigor that other parts of their lives suffer for it.

The last category which we shall discuss is the money whiz. These are inevitably the success stories among strippers, and most of them leave stripping at some point to either pursue other professional ventures, or to spend the rest of their time pursuing hobbies and passions since their financial affairs have been sorted out.

This category embodies the basic ideals of successful strippers, but you don't have to be a genius at money management to qualify for it. All you have to do is to have an end-goal in mind, and not burn through your money as if flushing it down the golden toilet would land you a ticket to Charlie's chocolate factory.

The successful stripper, on average, works far more than those of any other category—not because they *have* to, but because they understand that strippers have a shelf life of about a decade and wish to make the most of it. Instead of concentrating on partying away their newfound wealth, successful strippers turn that money back in and invest it into their own skills and education.

When dealing with house staff, successful strippers are fair because they understand the need for a happy professional network. They regularly share a part of their tips with the people who make their success possible, and do so ungrudgingly because they understand that they're receiving a service in return.

When dealing with customers, these strippers are well prepared but never brusque. If they need to establish boundaries, they do so in a way which impresses the need for that boundary without making the client feel insulted or slighted. As with other aspects of their **job**, these strippers understand that revenue flow depends entirely upon the satisfaction of the client— so killing the golden goose would be counterproductive. Successful strippers don't try to coerce or coax out any more money from their clients than they have earned through their work and time, but rather attempt to increase the quality of their own services so that clients would be willing to spend even more. Successful strippers also understand one truth better than most—who you associate with affects your own outlook and drive in life. Therefore, instead of getting closer with party-animal, perpetually-broke strippers, they form bonds with others who share a similar mentality—thus creating a network of successful and hard working personnel who would collaborate when necessary for mutual benefit.

Successful strippers also make it a point to maintain cordial relations with other strippers as well, rather than looking down upon or judging those less able or less fortunate. They understand that success brings enough resentment and roadblocks on its own, without adding fuel to that fire themselves. Instead, they attempt to build supportive surroundings with loyal co-workers who don't feel threatened by their success, but rather appreciate the successes brought to someone they consider to be kind, decent, understanding, and hard-working.

Chapter 4: Controlling Your Money

The most important aspect of a successful stripper's efforts isn't his/her behavior towards others or even to themselves, but rather their attitude to money. Since it's an untaxed income, with few ways for tracking tax evasions or enforcing other such legal deterrents, most strippers spend their entire cash earnings on trivial matters of short-term comfort. This attitude needs to be curbed right from the start—and if you're already given to it, it needs to be brought to heel as soon as possible.

The first major way to control your money is to stick it all in a bank account, which means you also have to pay taxes. Regardless of how you may spin it in your head, the deduction you face in the short-term will be nothing compared to your gains in the long-term—as you will realize within three years of starting on this path.

The second thing which you need to do is to curb your own expenditures, and set a limit for yourself. Since you're in a job where you may earn $700 one day and $1100 the next, if you're building your efforts well, the impulse to live within the means provided by these amounts is strong. However, as with any profession which has physical limitations, you need to consider the fact that you may have a single accident tomorrow which puts this life's earning potential far beyond your reach. So, you need to pick a decent figure—probably one which is congruent with the earnings of an entry-level recruit in any field of your choosing—and stick by it. To enforce this limit, you can either separate your bank accounts to create one for your savings and another for your daily expenses, or find a locked deposit financial instrument where you can keep depositing money for higher interest but can't withdraw it till the deposit matures.

Once you've put your saving implements in place, the next thing you need to look for is an opportunity to invest. Depending on your plans for the future, this opportunity can be either divided across two options or an amalgamation of both. If you decide to invest in yourself, search for high-value education opportunities. This could either be in the form of specialized vocational training, which may have great value in today's economy, or in high-value educational institutions where the cost of tuition is rather steep but the opportunities they offer are even steeper.

If you decide to invest in the future of your finances, the taxation of your income should now make it possible for you to own an investment portfolio. However, since novice investors have little experience in gauging the nuances of the stock market, financiers recommend beginning with reliable and reputable mutual funds. Since the analysts among such firms aim to balance out losses and gains across a variety of risk-based options, these mutual funds often turn a steady and respectable profit every year—thus allowing you to steadily build that money in your bank into a decent-sized nest egg. As this amount grows with time through the magic of compound interest, you will soon reach milestones where you may decide to leave the industry altogether to pursue other professional and personal goals. However, this is only possible if you don't have debt dragging you down.

So, if you have any debt to your name, spend the first few months or years clearing it right up—and avoid any further debts or loans like the plague. It's great if you have a credit card and participate in the credit structure of society as a productive member. However, avoid using any of your credit lines without exception. Even if you have to wait and save up for something big, spend that time and effort rather than taking a short way out that would nullify all future work and gain for years to come.

As long as you follow these basic outlines of savings, maximizing gain, and investing diligently, a period of ten years—the usual shelf life of a stripper from the age of adulthood at 18, and onwards—would be more than sufficient for you to break your first million and create a nest egg which could see you through many years of a future free from *having* to work for money. Instead, you would be able to choose your own path in life, with your own money, without having to depend on absolutely anyone else to support you in the slightest.

Chapter 5: Balancing Your Personal and Professional Lives

While this will be a relatively short chapter, the lesson within it is simple—don't stand on blind principle; listen to reason instead. Successful strippers reach the point of financial independence because they have the utmost confidence in their ability to pull through. Yet, this feat becomes far harder if the very group of people who know and understand us intimately, and who form the core circle contributing to our very identity—our closest friends and family—spend that entire time veering between immense emotions, and either disapproving or judging us for events or choices which they do not understand or of which they do not approve.

Therefore, the best choice for you would be to create an impenetrable barrier between your private and professional life, unless the circle of people around you is immensely and, often unusually, understanding. Try to ensure that the clubs where you work are sufficiently far away from places where the two aspects of your life may intersect, and never give concrete information about your inner life to colleagues and superiors.

While it may seem distasteful to have to lie about something which you aren't ashamed of, this particular need arises from more than mere ideology of honesty. As I mentioned before, successful strippers only treat this as a relatively short-term job which would allow them to build for their long-term future much faster through higher earning potentials. That means that this job will come to an end at some point in time, while those people around us will still be dear to us after years. Therefore, the priority in this situation becomes to create a balancing act which doesn't break any important bonds, or to potentially create a situation where long-term life quality is negatively affected by short-term moneymaking.

Another corollary to this—in case you have friends who do know about your profession as a stripper—is that under no circumstances should they be aware of your exact place of employment, or even enough vague details to be able to find that out for themselves. This is primarily to avoid a potential clash between those two worlds which would either force you to damage relations with your clients, or alter and damage the relationship and dynamics at play between you and your friends. Since your personal life is just as sacred as your work persona, you need to go through immense pains to protect both—lest you lose one at the cost of the other.

Conclusion

The world of exotic dancing is a heady and addictive experience. The easy availability of money, coupled with passions which naturally run high during such endeavors, make it one of the few most potentially psychologically damaging career paths that you may come across. And yet, if you have discipline and keep your feet firmly planted on the ground—it provides you with enough money to buy yourself out of the rat race and *still* save enough to start a small business of your own without added pressure of capital and funding.

As you enter deeper into this world, there will be several intricacies and moral nuances which you may have to adopt in order to stay ahead. For example, if the girls in your club provide non-sexual extras, you should consider doing so as well and performing them even better. Such extras are often the largest income in a day, since the client isn't ordering from the buffet of entertainment or even requesting a la carte—but rather calling out the chef and slipping him a hundred to provide something completely off the menu.

Also, there will be strict boundaries in and outside your work place which you need to stringently maintain in order to walk that fine line between entertainment provider and "alleged sex worker." One such rule among them is that you should never walk out or travel away from your workplace with a client, regardless of how you may trust them. This raises the wrong sort of suspicion, and if it unnecessarily leads to events of bad repute, the allegations may be enough to damage your future career trajectory in any direction.

Lastly, never be stingy while sharing your tips with others. As I mentioned, the house staff watches your back in various ways. And if it turns against you, there soon won't be much of a difference between you and the bottom feeder in the earning pool. Since you're banking on that influx of money to make your dreams come true, never be too uptight to forget the value of spending a little to make more money. After all, money is simply the vehicle to your diverse dreams— not the dream by itself.

Finally, I'd like to thank you for purchasing this book! If you enjoyed it or found it helpful, I'd greatly appreciate it if you'd take a moment to leave a review on Amazon. Thank you!

Printed in Great Britain
by Amazon

51748099R00027